DATE DUE

THE
AZTEC
INDIANS

THE JUNIOR LIBRARY OF
AMERICAN INDIANS

THE
AZTEC
INDIANS

Victoria Sherrow

CHELSEA HOUSE PUBLISHERS
Philadelphia

FRONTISPIECE: A solar disk, used by the Aztecs to tell time

CHAPTER TITLE ORNAMENT: A serpent-shaped gold lip plug, worn by members of the Aztec noble class

Chelsea House Publishers

EDITORIAL DIRECTOR Richard Rennert
EXECUTIVE MANAGING EDITOR Karyn Gullen Browne
EXECUTIVE EDITOR Sean Dolan
COPY CHIEF Philip Koslow
PICTURE EDITOR Adrian G. Allen
ART DIRECTOR Nora Wertz
MANUFACTURING DIRECTOR Gerald Levine
SYSTEMS MANAGER Lindsey Ottman
PRODUCTION COORDINATOR Marie Claire Cebrián-Ume

The Junior Library of American Indians

SENIOR EDITOR Sean Dolan

Staff for THE AZTEC INDIANS

TEXT EDITOR Marian W. Taylor
COPY EDITOR Danielle Janusz
EDITORIAL ASSISTANT Nicole Greenblatt
DESIGN ASSISTANT John Infantino
PICTURE RESEARCHERS Wendy P. Wills, Ann Levy
COVER ILLUSTRATOR Vilma Ortiz

7 9 8 6

Library of Congress Cataloging-in-Publication Data

Sherrow, Victoria.
The Aztec Indians/by Victoria Sherrow.
  p. cm.—(The Junior Library of American Indians)
Includes index.
Summary: Discusses the history, culture, and daily life of the Aztec Indians of Mexico.
    ISBN 0-7910-1658-7
    ISBN 0-7910-1963-2 (pbk.)
1. Aztecs—Juvenile literature. [1. Aztecs. 2. Indians of Mexico.] I. Title. II. Series.   92-18147
F1219.73.S53 1993   CIP
972'.018—dc20   AC

CONTENTS

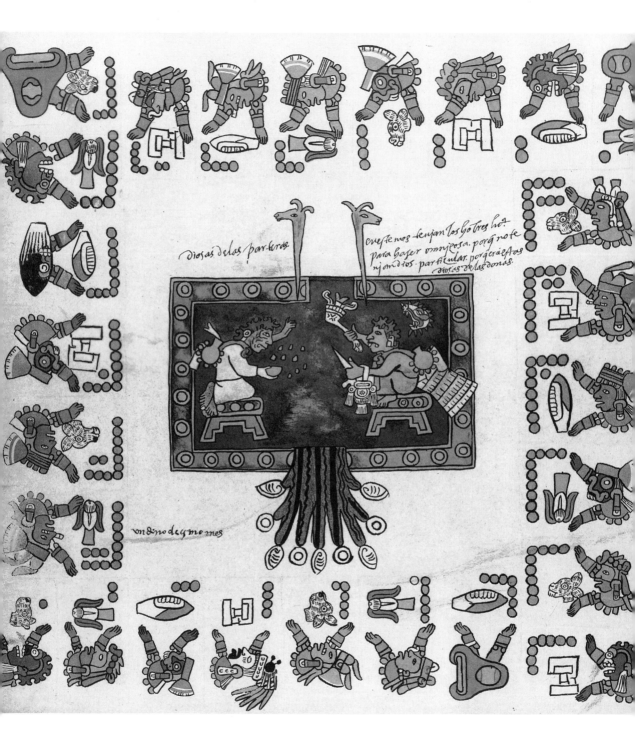

diosas de las parteras.

eneste mes tenjan los ȳotres hǒ.
para hazer vnujesosa. porȳ note
nj ondios. particular. porȳ eraestos
dioses de las donas.

vn dia no deg mo mes

The Aztec creator god and goddess, Ometecuhtli and Omecihuatl, surrounded by calendar symbols recording the passage of time.

CHAPTER 1

Five Worlds, Five Suns

Aztec legend says that the world has been created not once but five times. The first four worlds and their suns were violently destroyed. Powerful gods—the Lord of Duality (Ometecuhtli) and the Lady of Duality (Omecihuatl)—began by creating the earth. Two of their four sons carried on their work. These sons made still more gods, human beings, other living creatures, and the parts of the earth—mountains, waters, and valleys.

During the age of the first sun, called Four Jaguar, a god known as Smoking Mirror (Tezcatlipoca) ruled the earth. The people were giant sized and lived on acorns. This age ended when fierce jaguars ate all the people.

The world then had to be remade. In the second age, the sun called Four Wind was created, and the god of wind and air, Quetzalcoatl, ruled all creatures. Human beings ate piñon nuts, but then the people were changed into monkeys, and violent hurricanes destroyed the world.

Next came a third world, with the sun Four Rain. This world was ruled by the rain god, Tlaloc. Humans lived on aquatic (water-

The feathered serpent was a symbol of Quetzalcoatl, the Aztec god of corn and the fine arts.

grown) seeds until the world was destroyed by fiery rain. When this third world ended, people were changed into dogs, turkeys, and butterflies.

The fourth age brought a sun known as Four Water. The water goddess, Chalchiuhtlicue, was in charge of all things. People ate the seeds of a wild plant, perhaps an early form of corn. Then a great flood swept across the earth, and people were turned into fish.

Finally, the fifth world was created. The sun was called Four Movement, and the sun god, Tonatiuh, ruled the earth. For food, humans depended on corn. At this point, four suns and earths had already been destroyed. Would this fifth world survive? The Aztecs thought it might someday be destroyed by earthquakes. Then the world would be covered by darkness, and monsters would come down from the heavens to eat all the people.

The ancient Aztecs believed that the fifth sun had been created when one of the gods leaped into a fire. This god, whose name was Nanahuatzin, had given up his life to please the other gods. The Aztecs wanted very much to keep this fifth sun safe. To protect it, they devised a special religious service called a *New Fire ceremony*.

Every 52 years, the people held this ceremony. On the day of the ceremony, they put out all fires and threw away most of their belongings, including idols (statues of gods), cooking utensils, and hearthstones. Then they washed and swept their houses inside and out.

As the sun set, everyone climbed to the tops of the houses and walls. Women who were pregnant (expecting a baby) covered their faces with masks made of maguey leaves. Children, who also covered their faces, were told to be sure to stay wide awake and keep their masks in place. Everyone believed that if they fell asleep or took off their masks, the gods would turn them into mice. During the night, Aztec spiritual leaders climbed a hill near Tenochtitlán, the city that had become the Aztec empire's capital in 1325. There, on the hilltop, the priests offered a human sacrifice to the gods. They cut out the heart of a captive and then built the "new fire" in his empty chest.

Now, all the people held their breath. They were worried. If the fire blazed, all was well—the world would go on for another 52 years. But if the fire refused to burn, the fifth sun would grow dark, monsters would eat everybody, and the world would end.

But the fire always burned, and the people felt better. Now they could watch the next part of the ceremony, when the priests spread the new fire. The holy men dipped torches into the flames and handed them to the people who could run the fastest. The runners carried the flaming torches across the land. At each house, temple, and school, they used the torches to light new fires. And so another 52-year period of time began.

This creation story and the idea of the new fire ceremony were part of Aztec life hundreds of years ago. The Aztecs were a group of native peoples who lived in the central section of the country we now call Mexico. In 1325, a powerful group of Indian peoples called the Mexica (me-SHEE-ka) formed an empire with other native groups. Soon after, the Mexica renamed themselves the Aztecs, after a place called Aztlán, from which the Indians had traveled. The center of the empire's government was located in the Valley of Mexico.

The Aztecs did not have a written language with an alphabetic system. To show the history of their culture, they used *hieroglyphics*, a system of picture writing in which pictures were carved in stone. They built splendid temples and palaces and traded goods in

large marketplaces. They held grand processions and solemn religious ceremonies. Craftspeople, who were valued members of Aztec society, made beautiful things from clay, cloth, feathers, stone, turquoise, and gold. The Aztecs managed to do all this without the use of the wheel, metal tools, or such beasts of burden as donkeys and oxen.

When Spanish explorers came to their land in 1519, the Aztecs' capital, Tenochtitlán, was one of the greatest cities in the world. The

The Aztec capital Tenochtitlán, where ceremonies, games, and other public events were held.

well-armed, well-trained Spaniards conquered the Aztecs in 1521. Spain ruled this region for three centuries, blending its religion, language, and way of life with the ancient native culture.

The influence of the Aztecs can still be seen in the language, crafts, and foods of today's Mexico. About 1 million Mexicans speak some form of the Aztec language. Some Mexicans weave cloth or work at other arts and crafts using the Aztec style. Their work is a colorful reminder of a remarkable ancient culture. ▲

A solar disk, the Aztecs' calendar of the sun.

CHAPTER **2**

Ancient Tribes Form an Empire

Aztec history begins more than three thousand years ago. At that time, the peoples of North and South America had not yet developed alphabets, so there is no written record of those days. Historians have learned about them by going to the places where the people lived and looking for things they left behind. Jungle vines and blowing sands have covered over these ancient sites, but archaeologists, people who study the remains of past human life, know how to dig them out.

They have uncovered many signs of Aztec life—tools, pictures, calendars, tombs, altars, and houses. The historians have even found paintings and carvings that tell stories of these ancient people. They study these objects carefully, learning much about the way the Aztecs lived. They also talk with modern Indians to hear the old tribal stories that their

Temple of Quetzalcoatl at Tollan (Tula).

parents and grandparents have passed down to them.

Before European explorers came to the New World, many tribal groups settled in the Valley of Mexico. One of these groups was the Mexica, who had come from northern Mexico. Because the north was too dry to grow crops, the Mexica lived by hunting animals and collecting wild plants that were safe to eat. They lived in small groups and often moved from place to place in order to find the food they needed.

Between A.D. 1111 and 1325, most of the Mexica people left their desert homeland. They started out in Aztlán (place of the heron) and moved south. The Mexica traveled for many years, passing through places where other groups already lived. As they went, they looked at the strangers' ways of doing things, and they copied some of them.

The Mexica learned, for example, how to feed themselves by growing crops, such as corn, chiles, and tomatoes. Wherever they settled for a period of time, they started farms. They also began to make and follow calendars. The Mexica had always been very religious, and on their travels they were guided by their priests. At each of their temporary settlements, they built a temple in which to worship. Their most important god was Huitzilopochtli, the war god also known as the Hummingbird Wizard.

The Mexica wandered from one place to another, hoping to find a place to make their permanent home. The priests had told them that Huitzilopochtli would give them a sign when they reached the right spot. The sign would be an eagle perched on a cactus and holding a snake in its beak. The Mexica kept looking, but they saw no such bird.

When they reached the Valley of Mexico, they found people already living there. These older groups had their own political, religious, and social arrangements, and they did not welcome newcomers. They especially disliked the Mexica, whom they considered uncivilized invaders.

In the year 1325, a resentful tribe drove the Mexica into the swamps around Lake Texcoco, near present-day Mexico City. There, on an island, the people saw the sign they had been looking for—an eagle sitting on a cactus and holding a snake. So the Mexicans ended their long journey at a place they named Tenochtitlán, "place of the cactus in the rock." Aztec civilization began, and Tenochtitlán became its capital.

Living on this small island was not easy for the Aztecs. First of all, they were surrounded by many other more powerful tribes. Second, their island had no stone or wood from which they could build their homes and temples. But the Aztecs soon found ways to solve their problems.

Their young men proved to be excellent warriors, and soon they were being asked to serve in the armies of local rulers. They agreed, trading their services for building materials and other goods. Before long, the Aztecs were getting more things they needed by trading fish, ducks, frogs, and other lake creatures.

During the next century, the Aztecs became more and more powerful in the Valley. One of the ways they built up their military and political strength was by marriage. One Aztec ruler, for example, married a Toltec princess from nearby Culhuacan, which made the people of that city allies of the Aztecs.

When they first arrived on their island, the Aztecs built a small temple to Huitzilopochtli. As their population and wealth grew, they made this simple temple larger and much grander. In time, it reached a height of 200 feet.

The Aztecs connected their island to the mainland by building mud roadways across the water. When they had finished, they had three roads, one leading north, one south,

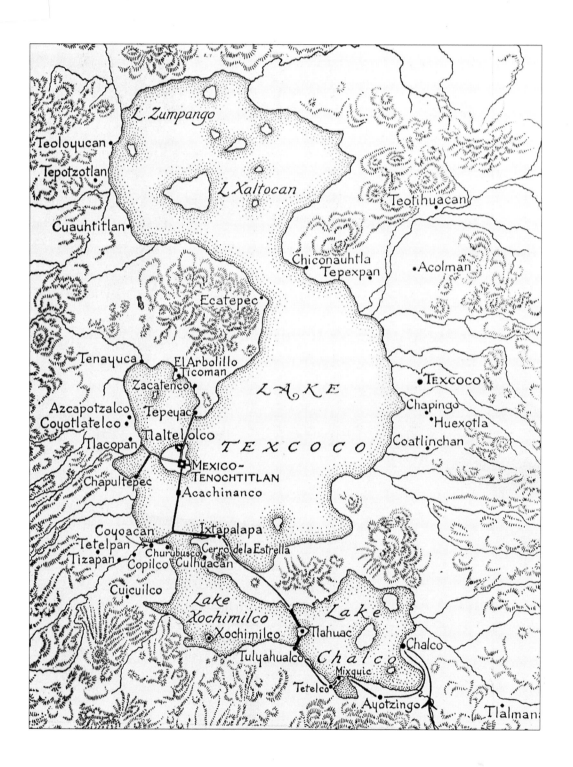

A reconstructed map of the valley of Mexico showing the lakes, surrounding mountains, and cities that became part of the Aztec Empire.

and one west. Now people could reach the island by canoe or on foot.

When they outgrew the living space on their island, the Aztecs came up with a clever plan—they created *chinampas*, or floating gardens, around the island. To build them, the Indians piled up layers of plants and mud in shallow parts of the lake. The chinampas did not really float. They were held in place at the corners by poles or by the roots of willow trees. Canals and walkways bordered these plots, where the Aztecs planted corn, beans, tomatoes, and flowers. On the firmer chinampas, the Aztecs even built houses.

The Aztecs had picked a good place for their settlement. It lay below snow-capped mountains, some of which rose to 17,000 feet (5,152 meters). Rain and melted snow ran down the mountainsides to fill the five lakes around the city. Today, these lakes are almost all drained, but centuries ago, they were connected to each other. This made it possible to move through them by canoe, which was good for the Aztec traders.

The lakes also supplied food—fish, ducks, frogs, and large salamanders—and grasses for building. The Aztecs harvested and dried the grasses, which they used to make thatched roofs, baskets, and mats. The

climate was perfect for farming, and it had natural springs for drinking water.

But the area also gave the Aztecs trouble: the water pouring off the mountains sometimes caused floods, which spoiled the crops. To solve this problem, in the mid-1400s the Aztecs built a dike—a wall of earth—across part of the lake. The dike sep-

A "good" farmer worked hard at his chores. (From the Florentine Codex.*)*

arated Tenochtitlán's part of the lake from the rest, which prevented much of the flooding.

In the late 1420s, the Aztecs became allies of the people of the powerful city of Texcoco. Then another nearby city, Tlacopán, joined Tenochtitlán and Texcoco. The three cities, known as the Triple Alliance, now ruled the Valley. Their partnership would form the core of the mighty Aztec empire. ▲

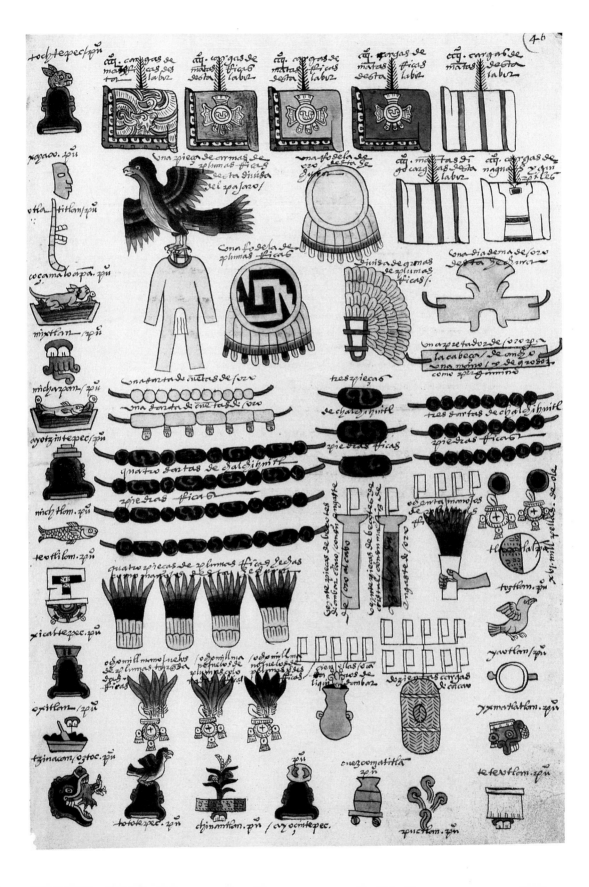

Clothing, costumes, jewelry, feathers, and food, sent to the Aztecs as tribute. (From the Codex Mendoza.)

CHAPTER 3

Aztec Society

In Aztec society, each person was expected to behave as well as he or she could. The Aztecs thought that life was like a journey along a narrow mountain path. Deep canyons lay on both sides, but if people stayed on a straight path and followed all the rules, they would not fall into the canyons.

Aztec parents taught children to obey their leaders, to work hard, and to be honest, modest, and careful. Each Aztec family was part of a social group called a clan. Within a city, each clan lived in its own district, set up around a temple and a school. At the center of the city was a public square, where people gathered for important events.

In the Aztec class system, a man's social position was usually the same as his father's. Wealthy people passed on their riches to their children, but the common people had nothing to pass on, so their children remained poor. There was an exception to this rule: a warrior who fought bravely and captured many prisoners could join the noble class and receive land and privileges.

At the top of the Aztec ruling class were the three emperors of the Triple Alliance. They wore beautiful clothing and crowns made of gold and turquoise, a polished blue stone. The rulers' grandly furnished homes were run by slaves who cleaned and cooked for their masters. To keep themselves entertained, rulers employed jugglers, acrobats, and jesters (clowns).

The rulers got their wealth from taxes and from *tribute*—goods they demanded from the conquered peoples of the Aztec empire. By the 1500s, that empire stretched from the Pacific Ocean to the Gulf of Mexico and contained about 15 million people. Each town in the empire was given a list of tribute its citizens had to send the ruler.

A tribute list, made up of hieroglyphics, might order a town to send jade beads, hundreds of bags of red peppers, bunches of bird feathers, and woven blankets. Another town might have to give dyes for cloth, military shields, beans, and silver.

In return for their wealth, Aztec rulers performed many duties. They had to organize wars and keep their lands safe from invaders. Sometimes they acted as judges, making decisions in legal cases. They also paid for and took part in religious celebrations. Each year, they passed out food, clothing, and other goods to the poor. In years when the crops failed, the rulers were responsible for feeding the hungry.

Below the highest rulers were the chiefs, who ruled the large city-states and smaller cities and towns. They, too, owned large homes and much land, and they collected taxes from the common people who worked the land. Like the kings, the chiefs inherited their positions from their fathers. They often served as judges, military leaders, and advisers to the kings.

All the other members of the upper class were nobles. These were wealthy landowners who served as government officials, astrologers (people who study the stars, then tell of events that are going to happen), scribes (people who kept records with hieroglyphics), and religious leaders. Some nobles held high military rank, and were expected to be courageous leaders in battle.

Between the highest and the lowest classes were the merchants and craftsmen. Merchants traveled long distances, trading goods and foods. They bartered (traded) their wares at large markets where people could trade for almost anything—not only food but jewelry, gold dust, tools, cloth, and pottery. Some of the merchants sold slaves, who were usually criminals or prisoners of war.

Every day, about 60,000 people came to the enormous market in the Aztec capital. It was run very carefully. Anyone who sold poor-quality articles had his wares taken away. Accused thieves were judged in a court of law right in the middle of the market. If a person was convicted of stealing, a judge might make him the slave of the person from whom he had stolen.

Aztec craftsmen lived in their own part of Tenochtitlán. They had only simple tools, but they made amazing things—gorgeous feather cloaks, impressive stone statues, and fine gold jewelry. Some craftsmen produced mosaics, pictures made with polished stones and gems. If he sold enough of his creations to the nobility, a master craftsman could become rich.

Featherworkers glued and tied feathers to items such as shields, headdresses, fans, and cloaks. They sometimes used turkey

A clay figure of an Aztec mother and child.

and duck feathers, but what the nobles liked best were the feathers of colorful tropical birds. The turquoise hummingbird and the quetzal were especially popular. Killing a quetzal was against the law, but a craftsman was allowed to capture one, pluck a few green feathers, then set it free.

At the bottom of the Aztec social ladder were the commoners. This class had three levels. At the top were farmers, fishermen, and makers of plain, everyday items such as cups or floor mats. Most of these commoners belonged to a *calpulli*, or district group. Each calpulli owned land, which it allowed its members to farm. When the son of a calpulli member got married, he was given his own land to farm.

Below these commoners were the peasants. They worked for members of the nobility, doing jobs such as farming, cutting firewood, and weaving cloth. All commoners were expected to work hard and pay taxes to the government. They were also trained to serve as soldiers. Sometimes they were ordered to work on a city project, such as building a temple, canal, or road.

On the lowest level of Aztec society were the slaves. A person was not born a slave— slaves' children, in fact, were born free. A person might become a slave for several reasons. If he was too poor to buy food and clothes, he might sell himself and his family into slavery to stay alive. Convicted thieves were often made into slaves, and so were people who did not pay their tribute or who owed money for gambling. The slaves themselves were not "owned" as people, but they had to work for their masters.

No matter what class an Aztec belonged to, religion was a major part of life. The Aztecs believed in many gods. Some of these gods had made the world, and others took charge of the events of daily life. The Aztecs' main god was Huitzilopochtli, the Hummingbird Wizard who had guided them to the Valley of Mexico.

Tlaloc, the god of rain and growing things, was also very important. So was Quetzalcoatl, the feathered serpent who gave art and corn to humans. Other less important gods protected special trades, such as those of the merchants and the gold workers. Still other gods were in charge of such things as salt, running water, and certain crops.

Boys of the noble class who were thought to be especially clever could be sent to a temple school when they were eight years old. There, the priests taught them how to make and read picture writing. They also learned religious songs and how to make medicines from herbs. Most of the boys' time was spent in prayer and in cleaning and caring for the temple and its artworks. They also had to keep the temple fires lit.

At the temple school, a boy learned how to be strong and live with discomfort. Sometimes, he and his fellow students fasted (ate nothing) for several days. At other times, they could eat only tortillas and water. They had to sleep on a bare floor and rise twice during the night to say prayers. In the morning, each boy pricked his tongue and ears with thorns, drawing blood to offer the gods.

Some priests were taught to be astrologers. These priest-astrologers were important men. Rulers asked them many things—when to go to war, for example, or whether there would be enough rain, or on what days to give sacrifices to the gods.

Astrologers gave advice to other Aztecs, too. People talked with them before taking trips, getting married, or starting important activities. Astrologers usually picked the day for a ceremony or public event.

Special public events were held when warriors came home from battle or when a new temple was dedicated to the gods. At these times, everybody in a city or town would gather in the central square to watch a splendid parade, sing joyous songs, dance, and

feast. Afterward, they would offer a sacrifice to the gods.

Human sacrifice was a very important part of the Aztec religion. This practice was based upon the belief that the gods had sacrificed themselves to create the world. The Aztecs also believed that every night, the sun god lost his flesh as he passed through the land of the dead. They thought it was their duty to sacrifice humans so that their flesh and blood would give the god a new body.

The Aztecs sacrificed great numbers of people, usually warriors captured in battle. When they dedicated the great temple at Tenochtitlán, for example, they sacrificed 20,000 prisoners by cutting out their hearts. They offered the rain god, Tlaloc, young

An Aztec mother and her baby receive advice from an astrologer. (From the Florentine Codex.)

children, because he was said to prefer them. The children were usually sacrificed by drowning. The Aztecs held a "new fire" ceremony, their most sacred ritual, every 52 years. At that time, they also built a new temple on top of the old one to please the gods.

Religious traditions, along with strict rules, kept Aztec society orderly. People understood what was expected of them and the work they must do. Living in a fertile land, with wealth from the people they had conquered, the Aztecs built up their own cities and way of life. ▲

CHAPTER **4**

Daily Life Among the Aztecs

W here and how an Aztec lived depended on social class. Commoners lived around the edge of the city, craftsmen nearer the center, and nobles next to the city square.

A commoner's hut had one room and a thatched roof. People of this class kept small gardens to grow their food and worked on plots of land owned by nobles. In their homes, a blanket hung across the open doorway. Placed around the room were the tools that the family used every day. These might include a farmer's digging stick, fishing nets, a loom for weaving cloth, cooking pots, baskets, and blankets. On the earth floor were mats that the women had woven out of rushes. Everyone—even the nobles—slept on floor mats.

Outside almost every home was a bathhouse made of *adobe* (sun- dried clay) bricks. To use the bath, a person lit a fire against the back wall. When the wall became red hot, the bather threw water on it, which made steam. Then he entered the hut and cleaned himself by beating his body with twigs.

Craftsmen's homes were also made of adobe bricks, but they were larger and better furnished than those of the lowest classes. No craftsman's house had more than one floor—only the nobles' homes could rise any higher than that. The nobles' palaces were built with whitewashed stone, and some had more than 100 rooms. On the flat roofs and in the yards of these homes, colorful flower gardens bloomed.

When the Aztecs first came to the Valley, they ate fish, frogs, tadpoles, lizards, and fish eggs from the lake. Later, when they learned to raise crops, they added vegetables and fruits to their meals. Their major crop was maize, a type of corn that grew well around the lake. They also raised beans, tomatoes,

A carved stone figure of a commoner holding a squash.

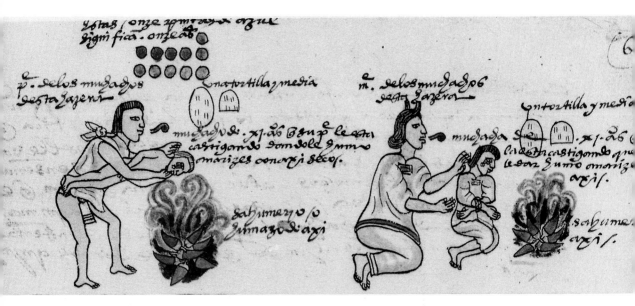

chile peppers, sweet potatoes, squash, and herbs.

For commoners, the morning meal was mush, a mixture of water and corn flour. Other meals included cakes made of water-fly eggs and steamed tortillas, a kind of pan-cake cooked on hot stones. Tortillas were sometimes filled with locusts or worms, sometimes with tomatoes or hot peppers.

Aztec nobles often enjoyed foods brought from other regions, such as cocoa from the south and turtles and crabs from the coast. A Spaniard who first visited Mexico in 1529, Bernardino de Sahagún, wrote about a rich Aztec's meal that included "two thousand kinds of food, hot tortillas, white tamales . . .

Parents punish their children by holding them near burning chilies. (From the Floren-tine Codex.)

turkeys, quails, venison, rabbit, hare, rat, lobster, small fish, large fish; then all (manner of) sweet fruits."

Aztecs washed their hands and faces before meals, which they ate with their fingers. At the end of a feast, nobles gave their guests tobacco to smoke in clay pipes and a chocolate drink topped with ground vanilla beans. These festive meals included entertainment by musicians, dancers, and jugglers.

It was the job of Aztec men to teach their sons and to provide the family's food and clothing. Women ran the house and cared for the children, especially the daughters. Women of all classes learned to weave cloth and prepare food, but noblewomen had servants or slaves to do the cooking, cleaning, and marketing.

Women married when they were about 15 years old. Men married at the age of 20, when they finished school. The man's family picked the bride, then hired matchmakers to make the arrangements. When both families had agreed, they called in an astrologer to set the marriage date.

On the wedding day, the bride's parents invited all their friends and relatives to a great feast. After the celebration, relatives painted the bride's face and adorned her with feathers. Then they carried her to the groom's house. The matchmakers performed the marriage ceremony by tying the couple's clothes together.

Men were allowed to have several wives, but most commoners could only afford to support one. High-ranking nobles sometimes had 3 or 4 wives, and kings might have 100 or more. Marriage was another way to make and keep political ties. A king would marry noblewomen from all the different parts of his region.

In the Aztec world, a person's hair, clothing, and jewelry sent out a message. A woman's hairstyle showed whether she was married or single. A man's hairstyle showed what kind of work he did. A farmer combed his hair one way, for example, and a warrior another.

According to Aztec law, commoners had to dress simply. Men wore cloaks made of rough, undyed cloth woven with plant fibers. These garments could not reach below the man's knees unless his legs had scars from war wounds. Women wore plain blouses made of two pieces of cloth sewn together. They wrapped and belted pieces of cloth around their waists to make skirts.

Nobles were allowed to wear cotton dyed in bright colors—purple, red, green, and blue. They could decorate their clothing with pre-

continued on page 49

SOPHISTICATED OBJECTS

During the height of their empire, the Aztecs created many powerful and delicate works of art, from magnificent palaces to elegant jewelry. They produced these things without the help of the wheel, metal tools, or beasts of burden.

Craftspeople, who were valued members of society, made beautiful objects from materials such as clay, cloth, feathers, stone, gold, crystal, and turquoise.

Religion was very important to the Aztecs. They created great stone figures of their many gods and goddesses, and they built splendid temples to worship them in. Many of the Aztecs' impressive artifacts can be seen today in the Museum of Anthropology in Mexico City.

An excavation site at the Great Temple of Tenochtitlan. Shells, clay masks, bowls, and other objects in this pit were offerings to the gods. The remains of the temple were found beneath present-day Mexico City. Excavations took place in the late 1970s and early 1980s.

A panel of skulls from an altar on the north side of the Great Temple. Three of the altar's sides are covered with these stylized skulls sculpted of stone and covered with stucco. The panel represents the skull racks, or tzompantli, on which the heads of those sacrificed to the gods were displayed.

Symbols of death, such as skulls, were common motifs in Aztec art. **Left:** *A human skull decorated with a mosaic of turquoise, iron pyrite, and shell. The Aztecs' preoccupation with death was intertwined with their belief that death was necessary for the creation of life.*

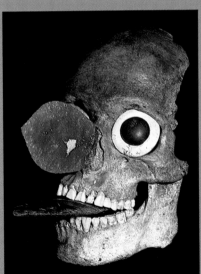

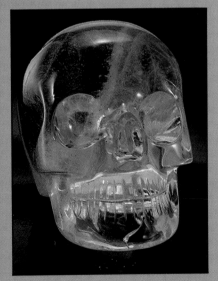

A human skull excavated from the Great Temple. Stone knives and eyes were inserted in the skull before it was offered to the gods.

This skull, measuring less than 4 inches in height, was sculpted from a piece of crystal, a glasslike quartz.

This gold nose ornament in the shape of a stylized butterfly (about 3 inches high) was found at the foot of a stairway in the area of the Great Temple.

Gold hummingbird ear ornaments (2 1/2 inches long) from Oaxaca, in a part of the Aztec Empire southeast of Tenochtitlan.

A two-headed serpent of turquoise and shell mosaic (about 16 inches long). Unlike the gold ornaments at left, which may have adorned statues of gods or goddesses, this piece may have been worn as a pendant by a powerful noble. To make mosaics, stoneworkers cut small pieces of jade, crystal, pyrite, shell, and turquoise, and fitted them into knife handles, helmets, shields, and skulls.

Jadeite (a type of jade) mask (about 6 inches wide) of the moon-goddess Coyolxauhqui. This mask was probably worn across the chest of a priest on special occasions. The most skilled artisans spent much of their time producing objects relating to the gods, goddesses, and rituals of the Aztec religion.

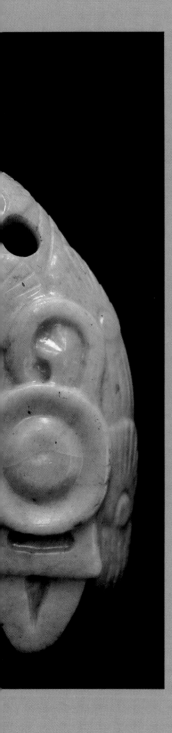

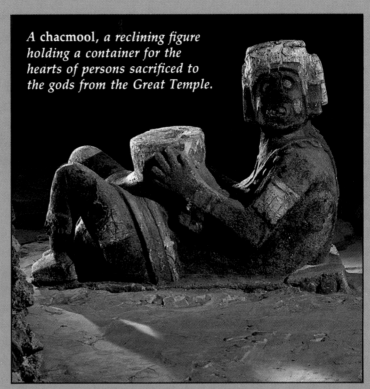

A chacmool, *a reclining figure holding a container for the hearts of persons sacrificed to the gods from the Great Temple.*

A mask on a ceramic vessel offered at the Great Temple. The strips that outline the eyes are characteristic of the rain-god Tlaloc.

This crouching stone jaguar, or ocelocuauhxicalli (about 7 feet long), served as a receptacle for the hearts of sacrificed persons.

This life-size ceramic eagle warrior was one of a pair flanking a doorway to the chamber where the eagle warriors met near the Great Temple. The eagle was a representation of the sun.

A painted stone sculpture, from the Great Temple area, of the god of pulque (a fermented drink).

continued from page 40

cious stones and feathers. People of the highest rank might wear cloaks with flowers, birds, and geometric patterns embroidered on them in gold thread. Noblewomen wore embroidery on their belts, tunics, and skirts. Their winter cloaks were made of rabbit fur woven with cotton.

Commoners were not allowed to wear much jewelry. They could decorate their ears, so most people pierced their earlobes and wore earrings made of gold or carved gemstones. Nobles could wear not only ear ornaments but gold headbands and lip and nose ornaments made of precious metals and stones. A commoner caught wearing this kind of jewelry could be punished by death.

Aztec children learned the customs of society when they were very young. Education began at home. Bernardino de Sahagún, the Spanish monk who arrived in Mexico in 1529, listed the rules that an Aztec nobleman would tell his son to follow. Some of them were:

> Do not sleep too much, or you will become a sleeper, a dreamer. Be careful . . . do not throw your feet or go jumping. . . . Do not speak fast, do not pant or squeak. Do not stare into another person's face. . . . When you are called, do not be called twice or you will be thought lazy. . . .

Dress carefully so you do not trip over your cape. . . . Eat slowly, calmly, and quietly.

Commoners' children learned to work at an early age. When they were five years old, boys gathered firewood and carried it into the house. By the age of 14, a young man knew how to fish in the lake and paddle a canoe. Girls of 6 were taught how to spin thread, and by 14, they could weave cloth and cook.

Children who did not follow the rules usually got a stern scolding from their parents. Young people who often disobeyed might be punished more harshly. Some parents beat them with a thorny stick. Others punished them by holding them over a pot of burning chili peppers. The smoke that rose from the chilies was painful to the eyes.

Aztec law said that children must attend school. In the evening, boys and girls between the ages of 12 and 15 attended a school called a House of Song. Here, they learned how to sing, dance, and play drums and other musical instruments. This meant they could take an active part in religious services in the temple, where music was important.

Boys began their formal schooling at age 15. Noble boys went to temple school, where priests taught them picture writing, history, law, religion, and the Aztec calendar. Commoner boys went to school to learn how to be soldiers. They also worked hard on jobs that helped the community—digging canals, putting up buildings, and raising crops. Girls of all classes usually stayed at home, where their mothers taught them how to keep house.

Aztec life stressed work and duty. But the people also had time for games and other fun. One of their sports was a ball game called *tlachtli*. In this game, players tried to put a hard rubber ball through a small ring. They could hit the ball only with their knees and hips. To keep from being hurt during this fast, rough game, the players wore leather body pads.

Most people liked to watch the tlachtli games, and many of them placed bets on the players. They bet all kinds of things— food, gems, clothing, houses, feathers, land, slaves, and cocoa beans, which the Aztecs used as money.

The Aztecs also played a board game called *patolli*. This was something like the modern game of Parcheesi. Players used beans as people now use dice. The beans were marked with white dots, to show numbers. Players tossed the beans to see how far they could move along a marked board or mat. Patolli was popular with Aztecs of all ages.

The Aztecs deeply respected their old people. No one was allowed to drink alcohol except the elderly, who could enjoy an alcoholic drink made from plants if they wanted to. And when old people gave advice or told stories, the younger people were expected to listen carefully.

Aztecs playing a game of patolli, using beans the way modern people use dice. (From the Codex Magliabechiano.)

All religions have special ideas and rules about death and burial. The Aztecs believed that people who died in certain ways—as in childbirth or in battle—went to live with the gods right away. Others had to spend some time in the underworld. Living people could help these dead by burying them with a lucky yellow dog, plenty of food, and other things they would need in the underworld. To help their dead relatives, the living also offered the gods prayers and gifts.

It was important that the Aztecs obeyed society's rules, to make sure they would get a proper burial. At every stage of life, the Aztecs knew what they had to do to please the gods and their fellow men and women. ▲

Tenochtitlan.

Aztec ruler Montezuma II and Spanish conqueror Hernán Cortés.

CHAPTER 5

Arrival of the Spanish Conquerors

As the 1500s began, the Aztec empire was at the peak of its rich and glorious culture. Its lands stretched from the Atlantic Ocean to the Pacific coast. Tributes and taxes came to the rulers from the 500 cities in the empire. Although members of other groups wanted to defeat the Aztecs, they were not able to outfight them.

The famous Aztec emperor Montezuma II kept his armies strong. He had been trained as a priest and astrologer, but he later became a warrior. When he took over as emperor in 1502, he moved into a grand palace and took several wives. The women he married helped make his position stronger; each was the daughter of a noble from one of the Aztec empire's important tribes. Montezuma enjoyed music, and he surrounded himself with art. He also found pleasure in his private zoo, where he kept exotic animals from all his lands.

During formal parades, Montezuma rode on a covered platform carried by four nobles. He wore a fabulous royal headdress made of long green quetzal feathers and studded with jewels. No one was allowed to look at the emperor's face. If someone wanted to speak to him, that person had to wear very simple clothes and no shoes. When the person talked to the emperor, another man told the king what the person was saying. Visitors did not speak to Montezuma directly.

But in 1518, Montezuma started listening to other people, for they had begun to report strange things. One old man told the emperor he had dreamed about the great temple in Tenochtitlán. It was "burning with frightful flames," he said, "the stones falling one by one until it was totally destroyed." An elderly woman dreamed that she saw "the great chieftains and lords filled with fright, abandoning the city and fleeing toward the hills."

What did these dreams mean? The worried

astrologers of Tenochtitlán talked it over with the astrologers of nearby Texcoco. They all feared that something terrible was about to happen. At last, Montezuma and the ruler of Texcoco decided to play a ball game to predict the future. If Montezuma won, everything would be all right. If not, the future would hold bad news. When the game ended, everyone looked frightened. Montezuma had lost.

Meanwhile, the Aztecs had been awaiting the coming of one of their important gods, Quetzalcoatl. Old Mexica legends said that this god had left their lands hundreds of years before. In the Aztec year One Reed, he was expected to return and take back his kingdom.

In the year 1518, messengers came to Montezuma's city with odd news from the seacoast: they had seen "mounds" on the ocean. The Aztecs thought this might be Quetzalcoatl coming back. They had no way of knowing that the "mounds" were actually sailing ships. They were carrying Hernán Cortés, a Spanish explorer, and 600 of his soldiers.

Cortés had spent the past seven years in Cuba, a large island off the coast of Mexico. In 1518, he set sail for Mexico, where he hoped to find great riches and land he could

The Spaniards, under Hernán Cortés, arrive on the coast of Mexico. (From the Florentine Codex.*)*

claim for Spain. His 11 ships held not only 600 men but 16 horses—animals no one in Mexico had ever seen. Cortés landed on the Mexican coast in 1519—which, by the Aztec calendar, was the year One Reed.

Cortés put his ships ashore near the present-day Mexican city of Veracruz. Because he thought the stranger might be Quetzalcoatl, Montezuma sent a group of his nobles to greet him. They gave Cortés an array of costly gifts and a complete set of the clothing in which they always pictured Quetzacoatl.

The Spanish explorer allowed the Indians to dress him as the god. They helped him into the jacket, the stone sandals, the jade jewelry, and the mask—the head of a snake studded with beautiful turquoise stones. Then Cortés fired one of his cannons. The heavy brass weapon produced a tremendous roar, a blinding flash of gunpowder, and billowing clouds of smoke. The Indians looked on with fear and amazement.

Cortés soon led his men inland, toward Tenochtitlán. Indian runners raced ahead of them, bringing news of the march to Montezuma. By now, the emperor wondered if these strangers really were gods. Still, he waited for their arrival, and he planned to greet them in a friendly way. As Montezuma waited, Cortés was meeting other Indians along the way to Tenochtitlán. Many of them hated Montezuma for making them join his empire. The Spanish explorer asked if they

A 17th-century engraving of Mexico City, formerly the Aztec capital, Tenochtitlán.

LA VILLE DE MEXIQVE

would march with him against the Aztec emperor. The Indians said yes. By the time he reached Montezuma's city, Cortés had several thousand new followers.

Montezuma treated Cortés and his men as guests. These guests, however, planned to rob their hosts. They would take all the gold and other treasure they could find. They also hoped to destroy the Aztecs' temple and turn the Indians into Roman Catholics like themselves. While the Spaniards were staying in one of Montezuma's palaces, they found a magnificent treasure room and took these riches for their own use.

Next, Montezuma led Cortés and his men on a tour of the city. They were impressed by the grand buildings, the huge squares, and the crowded market. But when Cortés reached the top of the great temple, he ordered his men to throw all the statues of the Aztec gods down the temple steps. The Aztec people who saw this were too shocked even to speak. After this, Cortés took Montezuma prisoner in his own city.

Soon Cortés heard that more Spanish ships had arrived at the coast. Spanish soldiers were on their way to arrest him because he had invaded Mexico without the Spanish government's permission. But Cortés went to meet the new soldiers and promised them

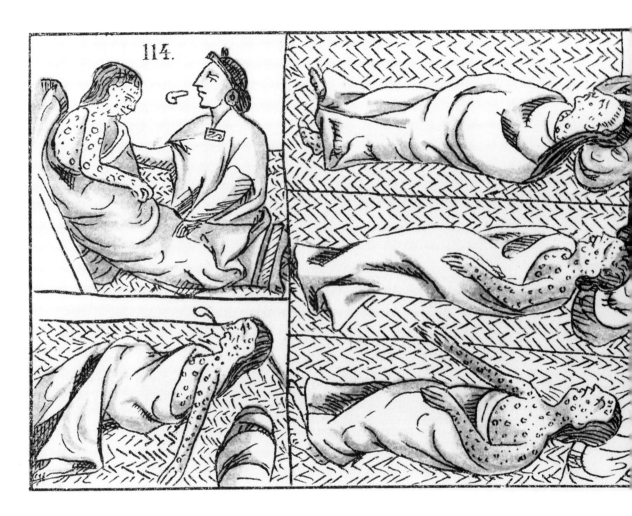

great riches if they would join him to fight the Aztecs. They agreed, and Cortés marched back to Tenochtitlán with 900 more troops.

When he returned to the city, Cortés found the men he had left there under attack. In the battle that followed, Montezuma was killed.

Smallpox, a disease brought over by the Spaniards, killed nearly half of the Indian population. (From the Florentine Codex.*)*

The Spaniards' supplies were running out, however, and they started losing the fight. On a rainy night in July 1520, Cortés and his troops tried to flee Tenochtitlán, but they wound up in an all-night battle with the Aztecs.

In this battle, known as the *Noche Triste* (Sorrowful Night), large numbers died on both sides. About half of the Spaniards were killed, along with some 2,500 of their Indian allies. With Aztec warriors still chasing them, Cortés and his men fled to the city of Tlaxcalla. They stayed there for about six months.

The Spaniards were gone, but the Aztecs now faced a terrible new problem: smallpox. This deadly disease was carried by the Spanish soldiers. It was new to the Aztecs, so their bodies had no defenses to fight it off. Smallpox killed Cuitlahuac, the king who ruled after Montezuma was killed. It spread throughout the Aztec capital.

The new ruler, Cuauhtemoc, worked to save his kingdom. He brought supplies into the capital and tried to persuade the Indians living on the coast to stay united with the Aztecs. Many of these people, such as the Texcocans, refused the Aztecs' plea. They decided to fight on the Spanish side.

In April 1521, Cortés led an attack on the

Aztec capital. About 900 men, including Indians, fought on his side. He also had 86 horses, 15 cannons, and 13 ships. The Aztecs killed some Spaniards and took others prisoner. They sacrificed about 50 Spanish prisoners—along with their horses—to the gods.

Cortés now decided to separate Tenochtitlán from the rest of the world. He placed ships in the lake around the city, so no food or water could be brought in. This lasted for six weeks. A witness later talked about this period:

> There was hunger. Many died of famine (starvation). There was no more good, pure water to drink. . . . The people ate anything—lizards, barn swallows, corn leaves, salt-grass; they gnawed . . . leather and buckskin, cooked or toasted. . . . Never had such suffering been seen; it was terrifying.

In July, after the city had become very weak, Cortés attacked. He had the best equipment by far. The Aztecs carried wooden shields and wore quilted cloth armor, but the Spanish used steel swords and shields. The Spaniards also fought to kill in battle. They did not stop to take prisoners for sacrifices as the Aztecs did.

The new emperor was taken prisoner in August, and the Aztecs were defeated. In just two and a half years, Cortés and his few hundred men had conquered a country of several million people. The country's whole way of life was about to change. Spanish laws, ideas, and goods soon spread through the land that had once been the mighty Aztec empire. ◣

An outdoor market in Xicotepec, in east-central Mexico.

Aztec Culture Today

When the Spaniards conquered Mexico, almost everything changed, including the makeup of the people. Diseases such as smallpox and measles came with the Europeans. Warfare had killed thousands of Indians, but the deadly epidemics that swept through the land killed even more. By 1570, the Indian population had been reduced to about half of what it had been when Cortés arrived in 1519.

Another change came about through intermarriage, which is the mating of people from different races or cultures. When a Spaniard and an Indian married, their children were called *mestizo* (of mixed parentage). In the

67

next generation, even more mixtures came about. There were marriages between mestizos and pure Indians, marriages between mestizos and Spaniards, and marriages between mestizos and other mestizos. In these combination households, the Indian and Spanish cultures blended together.

The Indians learned to use the metal tools that the Spanish had brought to the New World. New World farmers now worked with machetes and plows, which increased their crops. Wheels, carts, and wagons became commonplace. People began to raise animals their parents had never even heard of—horses, cows, sheep, goats, pigs, and chickens, which the Spanish brought from their homeland. The mestizos and Indians learned to grow wheat, sugarcane, olives, grapes, and other fruits and vegetables from Europe.

The Spaniards learned new ways, too. The Indians taught them to grow—and how to prepare—corn, chocolate, and tomatoes. Spanish noblemen bought fine works of craftsmanship made by Indian artists. While craftsmen kept busy, other Indians learned new skills, such as tailoring clothing in the Spanish way. They also began working in the gold and silver mines the Spaniards set up in Mexico.

A serpent-shaped gold lip plug, a type of jewelry worn only by members of the noble class.

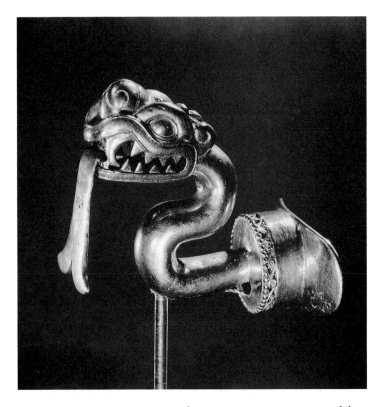

Some commoners began to grow wealthy by selling products to the Spanish. One such product was *cochineal*, a brilliant red dye made from dried insects. This dye was very popular with the newcomers, and a number of commoners made fortunes by making and selling it. The Aztec nobles bitterly resented these changes in the class system, but they could not do anything about the situation.

The nobles lost power after the Spaniards took over the leadership positions in Aztec society. Some Aztec chiefs kept control of their local governments, but they had to get

Spanish approval to make major decisions. As time passed, the Aztec class system, with its nobles and commoners, faded away.

Another major change was in religion. The Spanish sent *friars* (members of religious brotherhoods) to teach the Roman Catholic faith to all the people. The friars told the Indians that if they wanted to save their souls and stay out of hell, they would have to accept the Spaniards' religion. The friars also taught reading, writing, arithmetic, and music, but their main subject was religion.

The friars tried, but they could not root out the Aztecs' old gods. The Aztec religion, however, allowed the entry of new gods, so some Indians simply added the Christian God to the native gods. This upset the Spanish friars, and for many years, they fought bitterly with the Indians about religion.

The Spanish destroyed every Aztec shrine and artwork they could find, but they missed a few things. One was Montezuma's fantastic, feathered headdress. Cortés was so impressed by this stunning work of art that he sent it to his ruler, King Charles V of Spain. Charles gave it to his nephew in Austria, where it is now displayed in a museum.

Historians have found amazing objects buried under places where the Aztecs once lived. Where the great temple once stood in Tenochtitlán, historians have discovered a real treasure trove—everything from simple clay bowls to fancy jewelry, jade statues, highly decorated masks, and mosaics.

A Nahua Indian woman weaves cloth on a backstrap loom, a device much like those used by her Aztec ancestors.

These items give a small glimpse of the Aztec empire in its glory.

Other traces of the empire can be found among today's Mexican people. About 3,000 Aztecs who still speak the traditional Nahuati language live in the Valley of Mexico. Many Mexican citizens are descended from the Aztecs, and more than one million modern Aztecs live around Mexico City.

Although most of today's Aztecs speak the Spanish language and wear modern clothing, some of them still practice the old ways of doing things. For example, they weave cloth on the same kind of looms used by the ancient Aztecs. They often use Aztec designs to decorate their fabrics, mats, and pottery. The grand seal of Mexico has a center design that shows an Aztec eagle standing on a cactus plant, holding a serpent in its beak.

Aztec descendants also carry on their people's old ways of preparing such foods as tamales and tortillas. Even these words, *tamale* and *tortilla*, along with *tomato* and *chili*, are from the ancient Aztec language. Today these words are used not only in Mexico but also in Spain, the United States, and other countries.

Visitors to Mexico can still go to open-air markets, where some things have changed very little. People still barter instead of using money. And Indian craftspeople still bring their work to sell at the market, where native fruits and vegetables are also sold, along with prepared foods.

During the 20th century, native peoples throughout North America have gained a renewed sense of their culture and traditions. They have learned more about their past and have shared this history among themselves and with others. The story of the Aztec empire is an amazing and colorful part of the New World's heritage. ▲

PICTURE CREDITS

CHRONOLOGY

1325   The wandering Mexica people settle near present-day Mexico City and begin to create the Aztec empire

ca. 1420   The Aztec capital, Tenochtitlán, joins the cities of Texcoco and Tlacopán to form the Triple Alliance and rule the Valley of Mexico

1502   Montezuma II becomes Aztec emperor

1519   Spanish explorer Hernán Cortés and 600 soldiers land on the Mexican coast; the Spaniards capture Montezuma II

1520   Aztecs and Spaniards fight battle called *Noche Triste*, or Sorrowful Night; Montezuma is killed; Cortés flees Tenochtitlán

ca. 1520   Cuauhtemoc becomes Aztec emperor

1521   Cortés blockades the Aztec capital, allowing no supplies to enter; Tenochtitlán falls to the Spanish, who capture Cuauhtemoc; the Aztec empire crumbles

GLOSSARY

adobe   sun-dried clay, which the Aztecs made into bricks for building homes and bathhouses

calpulli   Aztec commoners' groups that assigned farming rights to the land they owned in each district

chinampas   layers of plants and mud in Tenochtitlán's lake that the Aztecs used to expand their living space

hieroglyphic   a system of picture writing used by the Aztecs

Huit-zilopochtli   the Hummingbird Wizard, the Aztecs' most important god

mestizo   a person who has one European and one Indian parent

New Fire ceremony   an important Aztec religious celebration held every 52 years

patolli   an Aztec board game in which beans were used the way modern people use dice

tlachtli   an Aztec game in which the players tried to put a hard rubber ball through a small ring

tribute   payment made to a conqueror by a defeated tribe or nation

INDEX

ABOUT THE AUTHOR

VICTORIA SHERROW holds B.S. and M.S. degrees from Ohio State University. The author of numerous stories and articles, she has also written 4 picture books and 20 works of nonfiction for children, including *Phillis Wheatley* in Chelsea House's JUNIOR WORLD BIOGRAPHY series, and *The Iroquois Indians* in the JUNIOR LIBRARY OF AMERICAN INDIANS series. Sherrow lives in Connecticut with her husband, Peter Karoczkai, and their three children.